ACTIVITIES FOR

FAST FINISHERS

Language Arts

by Marc Tyler Nobleman

SCHOLASTIC
PROFESSIONAL **B**OOKS

New York • Toronto • London • Auckland • Sydney
Mexico City • New Delhi • Hong Kong • Buenos Aires

Edited by Denise Willi
Cover design by Maria Lilja
Cover illustration by Jeff Shelly
Interior illustrations by Steve Cox, Jared Lee, and Mike Moran
Interior design by Melinda Belter

ISBN: 0-439-35531-1

Contents

Teacher Letter

About This Book

It happens to teachers all the time. A class is taking a test or working on a project and a few students finish sooner than the rest. They're sitting around, looking bored. What can you give them so they'll use what's left of the period in a valuable and enriching way?

That's where this book can be of help. It's full of high-interest activities that your students are sure to love. Does your class like crossword puzzles? What about word finds? Jumbles?

If so, they'll love the activities in this book, though none is a conventional crossword puzzle, word find, or jumble. In many instances, these exercises take those activities and add a twist—or just stand them on their heads.

Meanwhile, *you'll* like the activities in this book because they reinforce your curriculum by focusing on grammar and other language skills in fun, new ways. There are 55 one-page activities in all, designed to be worked on independently for an average of ten to fifteen minutes each. We've provided a checklist on the next page so you, and your students, can track which activities they've completed.

This book doesn't back down from challenging kids. It doesn't always go with the familiar word. It doesn't lose its effect if it makes a student want to look up a word in a reference source—in fact, all the better. It prefers not to repeat approaches, but if it does, then it must be for good reason! I hope you and your students enjoy this book.

— *Marc Tyler Nobleman*

Name _____

Student Checklist

Track Your Progress!

Put a ✓ in the box for each activity you complete.

FAST FINISHERS

Language Arts

Date _____

Name _____

Read, Write, and Solve!

What word means "able to read and write"? To get the answer, you'll need to solve the puzzle on this page. To begin, look at the word chart below. Only one of the three words next to each noun in boldface is a type of that noun. Circle it, then write it in the grid where it belongs. You'll know where to write the word because its last letter already appears in the grid. Write across using one letter per box. (The words won't fill every box in the row.) When you're done, you'll have your answer in the column down the center of the puzzle!

WORD CHART

tool	bench	cut	chisel
water	knoll	geyser	mesa
clothing	red	leotard	whistle
star	nova	comet	galaxy
house	mosque	kiosk	bungalow
color	shiny	ivory	striped
sound	thud	band	mouth
bird	ostrich	ocelot	orbit

PUZZLE: What word means "able to read and write"?

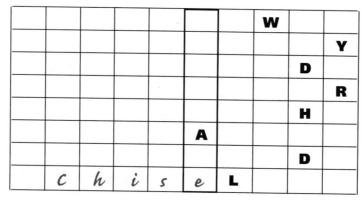

YOUR TURN

Use the puzzle's mystery word to write a catchy slogan that stresses the importance of being able to read and write.

_____

_____

6

Date _____

Name _____

FAST FINISHERS

Language Arts

Which Is Which?

It's a face-off! In each "competition" below, only one of the two words can be used as both a noun and a verb. Circle your choice, then write two brief sentences: one using the word as a noun and the other suing the word as a verb.

1. WRITE vs. DRAW?   Noun: _____
                            Verb: _____

2. SHOW vs. TELL?   Noun: _____
                            Verb: _____

3. DEPART vs. EXIT?   Noun: _____
                            Verb: _____

4. PLOT vs. IDEA?   Noun: _____
                            Verb: _____

5. LAWN vs. PARK?   Noun: _____
                            Verb: _____

6. BORROW vs. LOAN?   Noun: _____
                            Verb: _____

7. HIDE vs. SEEK?   Noun: _____
                            Verb: _____

8. LOSE vs. FIND?   Noun: _____
                            Verb: _____

9. SALE vs. SAIL?   Noun: _____
                            Verb: _____

10. TAKE vs. BRING?   Noun: _____
                            Verb: _____

11. DESTROY vs. RECORD? Noun: _____
                            Verb: _____

YOUR TURN

Stage your own competition! Find five more pairs of words—one that can be used as both a noun and a verb, and one that can be only a noun or a verb. Try them out on a friend.

FAST FINISHERS

Language Arts

Date _____

Name _____

Get in on the Action

Each sentence below is missing a verb. Circle any of the four choices that could work in the sentence. There can be more than one answer for each. We've done the first one for you.

TIP: Be careful with tenses!

1. My neighbor always _____ her dog in the morning.

   (walks)   grooming   (trained)   trick

2. Those birds always _____ overhead.

   flying   **sat**   **chirp**   **fly**

3. " _____ it, Michael!"

   stop   **hurry**   **move**   **ate**

4. Both of them _____ the puppy.

   buys   **name**   **named**   **will buy**

5. "Please empty the garbage and _____ the door on the way out," she said.

   close   **keep**   **shut**   **go out**

6. My favorite sport is tennis, but I also _____ swimming.

   play   **likes**   **am liking**   **enjoy**

7. If you _____ something in the dark, don't panic.

   feel   **went**   **hear**   **are**

8. The correct way to _____ a fire is written on that sign.

   start   **preventing**   **extinguish**   **prevent**

9. Don't _____ everything you read.

   be trusting   **believe**   **put**   **explains**

10. The children _____ noisily in the backyard and had a great time.

    played   **frolic**   **will stay**   **cavorted**

Activities for Fast Finishers: Language Arts Scholastic Professional Books

FAST FINISHERS

Language Arts

Date _____

Name _____

Whisper or YELL?

The verbs listed below belong in one of two columns: quiet words and loud words. Sort them into the correct column in the chart. Then go to the corresponding word finds and circle them. You'll find the quiet words in lowercase letters only in the quiet word find. The loud words in the other grid are in capital letters only. Words are across or down, not diagonal or backward. GO FOR IT!

VERBS	QUIET WORDS	LOUD WORDS
1. whisper		
2. yell		
3. mumble		
4. scream		
5. shout		
6. mutter		
7. murmur		
8. demand		

QUIET WORD FIND

```
W H I S P E D m o
w a h r D e a e M
h m u r m u r m C
i u e m u t t m U
s t M U T T E b R
p t m u r m r l M
e e m u m b l e U
r r Y u e s M u R
```

LOUD WORD FIND

```
T Y E s c r e a r
S H C O U T S C e
S a Y E L L T o S
H s S l l e s e C
O P S H O U T a R
U S R E y e l m E
R D E M A N D s A
Y E u y I o o u M
```

YOUR TURN

Find three other examples of loud or quiet verbs. If you need help, use a thesaurus.

_____   _____   _____

FAST FINISHERS

Language Arts

Date _____

Name _____

What the Action Is

Each noun below is followed by four verbs. However, the noun can only do three of them. In other words, the noun can be the subject for only three of the four verbs. Circle the letter of the verb that *doesn't* work with the subject. The first one is done for you.

1. ball	a. throw	b. drop	c. roll	d. bounce
2. window	a. break	b. see	c. open	d. reflect
3. tree	a. grow	b. fall	c. sway	d. chop
4. hand	a. stand	b. wave	c. grip	d. pat
5. star	a. twinkle	b. glow	c. explode	d. visit
6. dog	a. jump	b. yawn	c. throw	d. fetch
7. bucket	a. carry	b. leak	c. drop	d. fall
8. plate	a. hold	b. fall	c. eat	d. spin
9. driver	a. sputter	b. accelerate	c. brake	d. steer
10. asphalt	a. buckle	b. melt	c. crack	d. pave

YOUR TURN

Think of another verb that fits with each noun above and write them here.

_____

_____

_____

Activities for Fast Finishers: Language Arts Scholastic Professional Books

FAST FINISHERS

Language Arts

Date _____

Name _____

Can the Cat Act?

The word *cat* is a noun. But if you rearrange its letters it will become the verb *act*. Each sentence below is missing either a noun or a verb. You can figure out what the missing word is by rearranging the letters of another noun or verb in the sentence. Circle the noun or verb, then write the missing word on the blank line. We've done the first one for you.

TIPS:
- Do not count any helping verbs, such as be, can, or will.
- If a noun is missing, you will rearrange a verb. If a verb is missing, you will rearrange a noun.

1. At home, our _____*pets*_____ know they must (step) around the baby or she will grab them.

2. The wolf watched the stream _____ down the mountainside.

3. Vanessa is so excited to go to the toy shop that she _____ like a rabbit from the car to the shop's door.

4. The _____ of trainers will face its most dangerous job yet when it must tame the lion.

5. When opening the mystery crate, try not to _____ too loudly.

6. The _____ is planning to resign after tonight's concert.

7. If sales are down, the boss puts his head on his desk and _____.

8. My sister cannot _____ a moist piece of chocolate cake.

9. The _____ put down his brush and said, "That doesn't pertain to me."

10. "You will spot the _____ amid the clutter on the top shelf," my mother said.

FAST FINISHERS

Language Arts

Date _____

Name _____

Where's the Me?

A *pronoun* is a word that takes the place of a noun. In each sentence, one pronoun is missing. Pick any pronoun from the box on the right that fits, then put a caret (^) where the word should go and write the pronoun above it so the sentence reads correctly.

```
                    PRONOUNS

        their   her   she   his   me   theirs

              he   whom   it   I
```

1. Evelyn jumped after accidentally slammed the door.

2. Jackson couldn't predict how much snow would have to shovel after the storm.

3. Please help clean the house.

4. Molly's favorite color is blue, but most of clothes are red.

5. Don't know any secrets, but I wish I did.

6. Twenty students appeared in the school play and performed roles perfectly.

7. The teacher saw you do.

8. Her sandwich is much thicker than because of the homemade bread.

9. If these instruments aren't hers, then they must be.

10. You knitted a cashmere sweater?

Activities for Fast Finishers: Language Arts Scholastic Professional Books

FAST FINISHERS

Language Arts

Inspecting Adjectives

An *adjective* is a word that tells us more about a noun.
Look at each noun in boldface. What word listed near
each noun *cannot* describe it? Circle your answers. We've
done the first one for you.

NOTE: Splash does not
describe water. It is a sound
something makes when
it hits water.

1. **water**   deep / dirty / ice / (splash)

2. **voice**   quiet / deep / speak / squeaky

3. **lamp**   shine / street / antique / dusty

4. **path**   hidden / curved / dirt / direction

5. **beach**   windy / trip / private / tropical

6. **sentence**   opening / confusing / paragraph / important

7. **fence**   building / wooden / abandoned / unfinished

8. **star**   space / falling / north / distant

9. **time**   limited / no / enough / when

10. **child**   cranky / unruly / crease / wild

FAST FINISHERS

Date _____

Name _____

Language Arts

X Marks the Adjective

In this chart, nouns run along the top and adjectives run down the side. For each noun, put an "x" in the column of any adjective that could be used to describe that noun. Be prepared to explain your choices

	street	skunk	book	dinner	vine	friend	castle
inexpensive							
green							
long							
frightened							
hungry							
ancient							
confusing							
clever							
private							
mysterious							

FAST FINISHERS

Language Arts

Date _____

Name _____

The Difficul-Test Activity

Every sentence below includes one or more comparisons
using adjectives. But some of the comparisons are incorrectly
worded. Others are not incorrectly worded, but they can be
said another way. Circle these comparisons. Then decide
if you need either a correction for it or an alternative to it
and write it in the appropriate column. We've done the first
two for you.

SENTENCES	CORRECTION?	ALTERNATIVE?
1. Daniela has two sisters, but she is the (most old.)	*oldest*	
2. Yesterday was (more sunny) than today.		*sunnier*
3. This is the importantest rule of the game.		
4. She was the playfulest puppy in the park.		
5. The grass is always more green on the other side of the fence.		
6. Ms. Sapper got our class the more colorful piñata we'd ever seen.		
7. That part of the lake is the most deep.		
8. One cheetah was fastest than the other.		
9. The new student was the preparedest for the test.		
10. Objects in the rearview mirror are more close than they appear.		
11. Which American city is the farther away from the Canadian border?		
12. Mary was more sillier than the rest of her classmates.		

FAST FINISHERS

Language Arts

Date _____

Name _____

An Adverbially Tricky Code

Each of these sentences contains an adverb, but the adverb is in code. Don't worry about cracking the code, though. We're about to tell you how! Each adverb in italics is missing its "-ly" ending, as well as the letters "l" or "ll" from the main word. Plus, the remaining letters are scrambled! Figure out the correct adverb for each sentence. We've done the first one for you.

1. The fairies danced *foyju* every night. ____*joyfully*____

2. I am *uf* packed an hour before everyone else. _____

3. The young gorilla ran *fluapy* around his mother. _____

4. The maestro conducted the orchestra *tiriban* and received a thunderous round of applause. _____

5. A few kids didn't like the performance, but most of the class laughed *hiryecats*. _____

6. Tomorrow, I will *nafi* see the results of my audition and whether or not I made it into the school play. _____

7. The soldier stood *yola* by his commander's side.

8. The acrobat *lksfui* landed on the exact spot he promised. _____

9. We were *crtapica* asleep when a clap of thunder jolted us awake. _____

10. The sorcerer broke the spell by looking at them *cathnoiyp*. _____

Date _____

Name _____

Punctuation Situation

Each of the sentences or group of sentences below is missing one or more of the following punctuation marks: comma, colon, or quotation marks. Read each sentence and figure out which punctuation marks are missing. Put a caret (^) to indicate where they should go, then write the correct punctuation mark above the caret.

1. Jack needed help building a bookcase, so I said I'll be right over! He asked me to bring the following a screwdriver a hammer, and a box of nails.

2. On hot days only one thing would stop us from going to the beach crowds. Of course rain might also keep us away.

3. The letter began Dear Mr. President Thank you for your support.

4. I heard a strange scary howl last night I told my friend Jack over the telephone. I know it sounds crazy, but I swear it sounded just like a werewolf!

5. The line-up for tonight's show will be as follows Brenda the wonder frog Tulip the talking toucan, and Henrietta the hip hippo, the talk-show host said while looking into the television camera.

6. It's 300 P.M. This is when I usually like to snack on a piece of pecan pie and have a cup of tea. However today I don't want any pie.

7. At the rehearsal, the conductor gave us this schedule chorus meets every Tuesday band rehearsal is on Wednesday, and individual practice sessions meet on Thursday.

8. Remember this old saying An apple a day keeps the doctor away, the doctor told the little girl after the check-up.

9. Houston Dallas, and San Antonio are all major cities. However much of Texas is still made up of wide-open spaces.

10. This is the best way to describe the day of the race sunny and spectacular. Even so few people turned out to run.

Date _____

Name _____

A Highly Irregular Rhyme

A poet wrote the poem below, and he wanted it to rhyme. Why doesn't it rhyme in certain places? He forgot about irregular past-tense verbs. Help him fix the rhyme. Cross out each verb that has the wrong past-tense form and write the correct form above it.

Last night I had a great dream.

I jumped up and then I flied

Over land and through the clouds.

How? I really wish I knowed.

My landing was very smooth.

But down a small hill I slided.

This scared a small, quick creature.

I saw where it ran and hided.

What was that odd little beast?

To its hiding spot I creeped,

Peeking into the darkness

All I saw were toys it keeped.

Well, I thought they were all toys,

Until something burped and shaked.

One toy was really an elf

Surrounded by things it taked.

I did not speak, scream, or blink.

Down on my left knee I bended.

Just as I cracked a smile,

Straight to the forest it goed.

I started to follow it.

Then suddenly I awaked.

I stayed in bed in silence

Until a tiny voice speaked.

"Thank you for visiting me,

But I never can be catched.

Well, there's a way to do it

But it never can be teached!"

FAST FINISHERS

Date _____

Name _____

Language Arts

Sentence the Make

Latoya wrote a bunch of sentences on index cards—
one word per card. She was carrying them to show her brother
when she dropped them all! She managed to group the
words from each sentence together again, but she needs
help arranging the words in the right order. Write each
sentence correctly on the line provided.

TIP: Each sentence is
a statement; none is a
question.

1. passing barks my cars at dog

   _____

2. have family you nice a

   _____

3. newest are at the the the zoo animals penguins

   _____

4. you louder everyone so hear speak can

   _____

5. my clock got a he grandfather when this boy was

   _____

6. last I'm math I was year than at better

   _____

7. being good thank for a friend you

   _____

8. the gave free pitcher us tickets game next to the

   _____

9. father's air dream me for force is be pilot my to an

   _____

10. raisin shirt Frank's was as wrinkled a as

   _____

YOUR TURN

Take your favorite line from a song, rearrange the words, and see if a
friend or family member can figure out the title of the song it is from.

Date _____

Name _____

FAST FINISHERS

Language Arts

Places Trading

Each sentence below has a word that has traded places with a word in another sentence. To correct the error, you'll need to circle the word in each sentence that doesn't belong. Then, figure out which two sentences can trade circled words so they make sense. Rewrite each sentence with the correct word in its place on the blanks below. We've done the first one for you.

1. One of the lions escaped from the zoo but he was (splattered) safely last night.
   *One of the lions escaped from the zoo but he was **caught** safely last night.*

2. I always drink a glass of pizza before I go to bed at night.

   _____

3. The waiting room at the doctor's office is filled with old branches.

   _____

4. She got new sneakers this weekend, but by Monday they were already (caught) in mud. ___*She got new sneakers this weekend, but by Monday*___
   ___*they were already **splattered** in mud.*___

5. After the storm, we saw lots of broken magazines around the city.

   _____

6. On a long trip it's nice to have a good telescope to read.

   _____

7. Every time I have the show to eat chocolate, I try to resist and have a carrot stick instead. _____

   _____

8. He had never seen a meteor shower and was looking forward to seeing one through the book. _____

   _____

9. Some of the students brought in their favorite toys for urge and tell.

   _____

10. After winning the state softball championship, the team decided to have a victory celebration at the local water parlor. _____

    _____

Activities for Fast Finishers: Language Arts Scholastic Professional Books

Date _____

Name _____

Language Arts

FAST FINISHERS

Three Likes and You're Out!

Read Adele's report about what she did on her summer vacation. If she used any version of the word "like" incorrectly more than three times, she's struck out on her report! Circle any time she used like incorrectly. Did she strike out or did she make the grade?

What I Did on My Summer Vacation
by Adele Martin

Unlike the rest of my family, I never liked camping much—until this summer. I was forced to go on a three-day hiking and camping trip. Of course I expected it to be, like, the worst weekend of my life. I tried to get out of it but my mom didn't like that very much. "Like it or not, you are coming on this trip!" she said, smiling.

Once there, I started to feel differently. The forest had such a fresh scent, like nothing else I've ever smelled. I liked the sound of the babbling brooks. Every so often we sat on some rocks to rest. One time one of the rocks was, like, hot as if it had been in a fire—my dad jumped up as soon as he sat down! At night, everything was so tranquil. When I heard a strange rustling noise in the nearby bushes, I was, like, a little afraid, but it soon went away. We all slept very peacefully. A year ago I disliked camping, but now I say there is nothing like spending a warm night under the stars.

Date _____

Name _____

FAST FINISHERS

Language Arts

Turn! Run! Break! Fly!

Each verb in boldface below is accompanied by a group of words in a chart. The first column of words in the chart are prepositions and the second column are nouns. Draw a line between the prepositions and nouns to make a pair that will make sense with the verb. The first one is done for you.

1. turn   _on shower_
   _____
   _____
   _____

on	blanket
up	shower
over	driveway
into	volume

2. run   _____
   _____
   _____
   _____

through	mistake
over	choices
up	nails
across	stairs

3. break   _____
   _____
   _____
   _____

into	ice
down	mob
up	laughter
through	wall

4. fly   _____
   _____
   _____
   _____

off	style
in	sunset
into	handle
by	night

Date _____

Name _____

Language Arts Smarts

How much do you know about the English language? Cross off the portions of the statements below that are false. In other words, make them true! In the blanks, explain why the statement you crossed out was false. If the statement is entirely true, circle it.

1. Clan, crevice, constable, and cower are all examples of nouns.

_____

2. The sentence, "You couldn't help but doubt such a story," is not an example of a double negative.

_____

3. The words title, variety, spider, and iodine all have the long i vowel sound.

_____

4. The pronoun, adverb, preposition, and comma are all parts of speech.

_____

5. The words knight, pirate, gladiator, and viking are not commonly capitalized. _____

6. The letters a, e, i, o, u, and y are always vowels.

_____

7. Sagas, parables, and fables are all types of stories. _____

_____

8. Homogenized, serialized, pasteurized, and anesthetized are all adjectives that can be used to describe kinds of milk. _____

_____

9. These letters are all consonants: c, d, i, k, l, m, v, and x.

_____

10. The grammar and punctuation are correct in this sentence, which features a list of the following animals: Goose, moose, sheep, and deer.

_____

FAST FINISHERS

Language Arts

One Letter Short

One word in each of the sentences below is incorrectly spelled because it's missing a letter. Can you figure out which word it is and which letter is missing in each example? Put a caret (^) where the letter should go, then write the missing letter next to each sentence in the right-hand column of the chart.

SENTENCE	MISSING LETTER
1. The newscaster reported that a group of jakals escaped from the zoo at about six o'clock this morning, but assured viewers that nobody is in any danger.	
2. When Quentin drove, nobody thought he knew which rout to take, but he soon showed just how good his memory was when he zoomed off the correct exit without needing help.	
3. It was exactly five years ago today that a quartet of scientists uncovered the skeleton of a previously unknown Jurasic dinosaur about the size of a horse.	
4. Even though they wore disguises, the king and queen expected to be recognized as they walked quietly among the citizen of their kingdom to observe how they lived.	
5. The most amazing thing about the novel is that all of us liked the plot and just about every one of the characters—exept the protagonist!	
6. A jitery Zelda couldn't find her guitar, xylophone, or viola anywhere despite the fact that she turned the entire house upside down looking for the instruments.	
7. You can buy suculent squashs, juicy watermelons, and plump nectarines at the farmers' market.	
8. A bookeeper has the very important job of keeping track of people's money and daily business affairs.	

FAST FINISHERS

Language Arts

Date _____

Name _____

A Misspell Spell

A mischievous young magician accidentally jumbled the vowels on signs all over town. Undo his spell so the signs are readable again by figuring out which vowels he switched around. Write your answers (including the vowels that were switched) in the blanks. We've done the first one for you.

HINT: Be warned! Each sign has a different jumble!

1. Froo Pirkung = _Free Parking_ (a became i, e became o, i became u)
   _____

2. Ipan 24 Hiers = _____
   _____

3. Eno Sazo Fats Ull = _____
   _____

4. Pliesi Drovi Cerifally = _____
   _____

5. Onnuvarsory Sola = _____
   _____

6. Tackot Wanduw = _____
   _____

7. Wulcimu ti Ior Schiil = _____
   _____

8. Kuup Yeir Tewn Cluon = _____
   _____

9. Faxud Whalu Yei Woat = _____
   _____

10. Wark Zani = _____
    _____

YOUR TURN

Create your own jumble like the ones above. See if your classmates can figure out what your sign says and which vowels you switched around.

FAST FINISHERS

Language Arts

Date _____

Name _____

Letter Twins Go Missing

Each of these words begins and ends with the same letter—
but that letter has _isappeare_! Determine the correct missing
letter, then spell the word in the chart. There is only one correct
letter for each, except for one example, which has two correct answers.

WORD	MISSING LETTER	CORRECTLY SPELLED
1. _isappeare_		
2. _rai_		
3. _atio_		
4. _scap_		
5. _illo_		
6. _ainstrea_		
7. _evive_		
8. _inemati_		
9. _ivi_		
10. _rea_		
11. _aya_		
12. _ada_		

YOUR TURN

Several of the words above have more than letter twins—they're
palindromes. Palindromes are words or sentences that read the same
way forward or backward. Which are they? Circle them. Then try to write
a short palindrome sentence.

Date _____

Name _____

Strange Spelling Bee

This year, the Norton Elementary School spelling bee is featuring some of the hardest words to spell. Each student spelled each word wrong by at least one letter. How soon were the words spelled wrong? Rank them from 1 (mistake in the first letter) to 12 (mistake in the twelfth letter). We've done the first one for you.

INCORRECTLY SPELLED WORD	CORRECTLY SPELLED WORD	1ST LETTER WRONG	RANK (1–12)
niether	neither	2nd letter "i" should be "e"	2 (earliest mistake)
dunjeon			
absense			
associatian			
governer			
correspondance			
emphibian			
environmentul			
thesauris			
boomarang			
chlorophill			
nesessary			

Activities for Fast Finishers: Language Arts   Scholastic Professional Books

FAST FINISHERS

Language Arts

Date _____

Name _____

Blurring the Lines

The list below contains some words that are spelled incorrectly. Circle only the words that are spelled correctly. Then use a pencil to write those words in the 50-box grid, one letter per box. How will you know where they belong? Two letters are provided in the grid to start you off. When filled in correctly, the last letter of each word is also the first letter of the following word (except the first and last words!), as in the example. Each correctly spelled word has only one possible place within the boxes.

Example: If the first word is "explain" and the second word is "narrate," the words would be placed in the row like this:

e	x	p	l	a	i	n	a	r	r
a	t	e							

WORD LIST

heyday	rancid	napsack	plunder
dabbel	naive	nymph	existance
yearn	drivel	havock	rinocerous
dumbfounded	playright	rhthym	lexicon

GRID

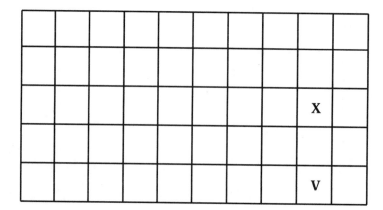

FAST FINISHERS

Language Arts

Date _____

Name _____

No Nonsense!

Which word in each group becomes nonsense if you replace each of its vowels with "o"? Write that word in the blanks. Don't worry if you come across a word that already has an "o" in it. You are only changing the *other* vowel or vowels. (After all, you can't change an "o" to an "o"!)

Example: luck, lint, into, drip   *lint* _____

The word you would write on the blank is **lint** because **lont** is not a word. The other three all make words when you replace their non-"o" vowels with "o": **lock, onto, drop.**

TIP: Don't count "y" as a vowel in this exercise.

1. rose, flour, ward, moan   _____

2. burn, creek, oboe, flip   _____

3. mast, pole, tell, open   _____

4. grass, plant, weed, farm   _____

5. click, knack, snap, blab   _____

6. sent, list, sang, pets   _____

7. leap, say, pear, trail   _____

8. reef, button, rout, must   _____

9. noun, rude, finale, steal   _____

10. tea, ugly, type, ship   _____

YOUR TURN

Create a series of words like the ones above. See if your classmates can figure out which word would be the nonsense word when its vowel is replaced with an "o."

Date _____

Name _____

FAST FINISHERS

Language Arts

Like Two Peas in a Pod

For each group below, circle any vowel pair that can form a common word if put between the consonants, like "two peas in a pod." There can be more than one correct answer. We've done the first one for you.

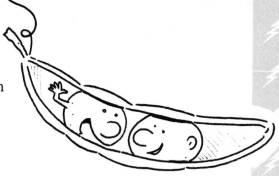

1. dt	*duet, diet*	(ue)	ae	(ie)	oe
2. rt		io	oo	ae	ea
3. st		ai	ea	ie	oo
4. lr		ai	ee	ou	ia
5. mt		oo	ea	ai	ue
6. dl		ue	ea	ua	ia
7. sp		ea	ee	ou	oa
8. bk		ue	oo	ea	ai
9. pl		oo	ee	ai	oi
10. dd		ee	ie	ea	oo
11. tl		oi	ia	ai	ue
12. mn		ea	oo	ai	oe
13. sm		oo	ai	ea	ue
14. pr		ea	ue	oo	ee
15. rr		oo	ue	ea	ia

Date _____

Name _____

Animal Spies

If you study each list of animals below you'll discover one more hidden animal. How? By combining the first letters of each animal into a new word. But beware! Two animal spies have crept into each group—and they must be removed to correctly spell the hidden animal. Circle both sneaks in each group and write them in the chart below. Then write the hidden animal in the center column. We've done the first one for you.

THE LIST	IF YOU REMOVE	HIDDEN ANIMAL
1. Bear, (camel,) (rhinoceros,) urodele, llama, lion	camel, rhinoceros	b-u-l-l
2. narwhal, walrus, eagle, antelope, seal, echidna, lemur, grasshopper		
3. porpoise, earthworm, lion, louse, giraffe, impala, cougar, aardvark, newt		
4. gnu, asp, zebra, elk, ibis, leopard, ladybug, eel, armadillo		
5. panther, orca, moth, rabbit, catfish, urchin, panda, iguana, nightingale, anteater, elephant		
6. chipmunk, robin, ibex, snake, crab, kangaroo, egret, coyote, tuna		
7. toucan, otter, swan, sheep, tapir, rat, inchworm, chimpanzee, hyena		
8. squid, albatross, lemming, auk, spider, manatee, muskrat, alligator, needlefish, dingo, emu, raven		
9. llama, osprey, bat, squirrel, tiger, python, ermine, wombat, raccoon		
10. aardvark, mustang, owl, fox, lion, eagle		

Date _____

Name _____

FAST FINISHERS

Language Arts

E-I-E-I-O

The vowels "e," "i," and "o" are the stars of the show in
the song "Old McDonald Had a Farm." They're the
stars here, too. The consonants in each example are all
mixed up. But they can be made into a word if you
unscramble them and add double vowels—either "ee," "ii,"
or "oo." Only one of these double vowels works for each jumble.
We've done the first one for you.

JUMBLE	WORD
1. tr ➡	*root*
2. nm ➡	_____
3. sm ➡	_____
4. rei ➡	_____
5. gil ➡	_____
6. lchs ➡	_____
7. sykp ➡	_____
8. nkgiln ➡	_____
9. seld ➡	_____
10. gnks ➡	_____
11. nuq ➡	_____
12. waha ➡	_____

YOUR TURN

Create three jumbled consonants like the ones above and see if your
classmates can figure out the missing double vowels and the word they
create.

FAST FINISHERS

Language Arts

A Classics Problem

You've just been handed a stack of classic children's book titles that
have been renamed. Your boss wants to know the original title of
each children's classic and to make sure the new titles are spelled
and punctuated correctly before they are printed in a catalogue. But
you have a problem: The original list of titles was accidentally thrown away.
Figure out the original title based on the meanings, then circle any misspellings
or incorrect punctuation you find. We've done the first one for you.

NEW TITLE	ORIGINAL TITLE
1. The Fealine in the Headwear	*The Cat in the Hat*
2. The Chirping Insect in the Central Tourist Sight of a Big American City	
3. Small Residance on the Flat Land in the Middle of the Country	
4. The Place Creatures Who Are Not Well Behaved Live	
5. The Large Cat, the Woman With Supernaturel Powers, and the Clothes Closet	
6. Farewell for the Evening, Earth's Satelite	
7. The Insect With a Strong Apetite	
8. The Small Locomotave That Was Able	
9. The Twenty-Four-Hour Period of Cold Precipitashun	
10. The Tall Plant That Is Very Jenerous	
11. Predict the Amount of Effection I Have for You	
12. Fast Train to the Artic	

YOUR TURN

Rename a favorite book of yours. Avoid books with proper names in the
title (such as *Curious George*) because there are usually no other words for
them!

Date _____

Name _____

Language Arts

Double Take

Below is a series of incomplete words. Each word is missing a set of double letters that will make the word whole. Write them in the center column of the chart. (There can be more than one set per incomplete word.) Then, write the words formed with the double letters on the right-hand side of the chart.

INCOMPLETE WORD	MISSING DOUBLE LETTER(S)	WORD(S) FORMED
1. bu??le		
2. a??ount		
3. pu??le		
4. j??r		
5. ba??le		
6. o??		
7. si??ing		
8. fu??y		
9. p??l		
10. e??		

YOUR TURN

Think of three other words with double letters. Then see if any other double letter could replace them and make another.

34

FAST FINISHERS

Language Arts

Date _____

Name _____

Letter Lottery

Each word below is followed by a choice of three letters. Only one of the three can form a new word (or words) when the letters of the original word are rearranged and the extra letter is added to them. Write the correct letter, then write the new word or words it forms. We've done the first one for you.

ORIGINAL WORD	LETTER CHOICES	CORRECT LETTER	NEW WORD
1. raid	e, o, w	*o*	*radio*
2. apes	f, k, m		
3. echo	d, i, r		
4. lamp	e, o, t		
5. grow	a, n, u		
6. half	a, g, s		
7. lips	l, y, z		
8. cool	a, i, r		
9. ride	o, u, v		
10. large	m, g, p		

YOUR TURN

Create three more exercises like these and try them with your classmates.

FAST FINISHERS

Language Arts

Date _____

Name _____

TIP: None of the pies is apple!

Pieces of Pie

There are six mystery "pies" on this page. Each pie is cut into pieces. To figure out what type of pie each one is, you'll need to work with the letters and letter combinations at the bottom of the page. Using a pencil, test these combinations in the pie slices, and rework them until the right type of pie is spelled out for each one. Cross off each letter or combination after you use it, since each is used only once. You may not rearrange a letter combination. (If it's "au," you can't make it "ua.") We've done the first one for you.

1. Pie with three slices:

pecan

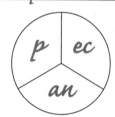

2. Pie with four slices:

_____

3. Pie with five slices:

_____

4. Pie with six slices:

_____

5. Pie with four slices:

_____

6. Pie with five slices:

_____

LETTERS AND LETTER COMBINATIONS

PU	UE	~~P~~	ST	~~EC~~	LI	ST	PK	RR
WB	EY	IN	ON	BE	RY	BL	M	RA
Y	CR	BO	~~AN~~	AM	K	ER	E	ME

FAST FINISHERS

Language Arts

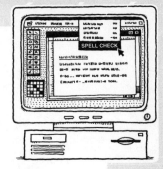

Double Check

It's easy to think that when you work with a computer, you can't
misspell a word as long as you use the spell-check feature. But,
even computers make mistakes, especially when they come across
homophones—words that sound alike but have different spellings
and meanings. Below is a list of sentences that have been spell-checked by
a computer. Circle the incorrect homophones the computer missed. Some
sentences have more than one. Write the correct word or words on the line.

1. The shellfish had such a strong mussel that it couldn't be pride open with
   a knife. _____

2. Losing the soccer championship to a team that had an inferior record last
   season was a lessen in overconfidence for our team. _____

3. Queen Ima Badrula's rein ended abruptly when her people decided they
   wanted a new sovereign and overthrew her. _____

4. I felt sorry for the oxen in the field because they kept throwing their heads
   back in an attempt to loosen the yolks that hung heavily around their
   necks. _____

5. If you want to take photographs of an animal in the wild, you knead to be
   absolutely stationery or else you'll scare your subjects away.

   _____

6. Turns are beautiful birds to watch, especially when they are soaring over
   the crashing surf at the beach. _____

7. We didn't discover any buried treasure on the beach, but we did fined a
   broken peace of medal, which we first thought was gold. _____

8. When you complement a person on a job well done, don't expect one in
   return. _____

9. The steaming hot muffins were loaded with small, sweet currents, which
   gave off a wonderful sent. _____

10. The Army Core of Engineers has worked hard to build bridges, tunnels,
    and highways so Americans can travel moor easily. _____

Date _____

Name _____

FAST FINISHERS

Language Arts

Word Magic

Anagrams are words that contain the exact same letters, but in different orders. For example, *sole/lose* and *arms/rams* are anagrams. Look at the sentences below. Which two words in each sentence are anagrams of one another? Circle them. We've done the first one for you.

1. (Poles) were set up all the way down the (slope) to guide skiers.

2. Have you ever seen a movie where rats were the star of the show?

3. The deer stepped gingerly toward the patch of weeds and tasted the reed.

4. We read a book about a brave woman who traveled across the ocean alone in a canoe.

5. The little boy couldn't keep himself from taking a peek to see if there were any shiny wrapped gifts for him in the shopping bag.

6. The museum curator could not predict how he would react when he opened the crate of mummies from Egypt.

7. When I helped my parents build a stone wall in our yard, I took notes so I'd remember how to do it on my own one day.

8. The new game was unusual because anyone who hit the ball into the net didn't lose any points but was rewarded with ten extra points.

9. In my history class we learned how some explorers would ignore a region if they didn't think they could find gold there.

10. The plants in our garden might be in danger from insects and other pests.

YOUR TURN

Write your own sentence that includes anagrams. Have a friend or family member find the anagrams.

Date _____

Name _____

Word Hide

A word find is a puzzle in which you circle words that are hidden in a grid of letters. This puzzle is the reverse—it's a word *hide*! Read the rules to find out how to hide this list of mysterious words in the grid below.

spooky	twisted	legend	footprint	strange
magic	cobweb	inspect	sleuth	phantom

RULES

- To hide each word, you'll need to look for letters of the word that are already in the grid. For example, to hide the word "talk" find the letters "t," "a," and "l" in a row. If there's an empty box after the "l," you can write in the letter "k" to finish and hide the word.
- You cannot change any letters that are already in the grid.
- Words can be written either across or down, not backward or diagonally.
- Each word has only one correct hiding place.
- Some boxes will still be empty when you're done.

	v	b	o			g	e		d		a		
	f		a		f	o	o	t	p		x		t
a			s		f		o	t	p	r			c
n	s	z		f		l	e	u				i	o
	t	o			e		m	a	g		l	p	
o		t		o			n		t	i	h	t	w
m	a		t	r		n		e	o	n	a	e	
	n		d		a	t	w		m			a	
		s		r		p		e		p	y	t	
g	m	b		i	t	i	n		p		e	t	
h	a		o			j	u			c	o	s	l
		k			v			r	o		m		
		t	w			t		t				c	
	c	o			b			s	t	e	r	o	
l	e			d	n			p		o		y	

Date _____

Name _____

Rhyme Is Reason

Every list below is missing a one-syllable word.
At first glance, there is no single correct answer. To complete
each group of words, think of what each list of words is about.
Then choose a word to fit that list that also rhymes with the other
mystery words in the group. Write your answers on the lines and
tell what each list of words is about in parentheses. We've done
the first one for you.

GROUP 1

Connecticut, New Mexico, ___Maine___ *(U.S. states)*

car, boat, ___plane___ *(forms of transportation)*

heart, lungs, ___brain___ *(parts of the body)*

> **DON'T FORGET:**
> The mystery words in
> each group must rhyme
> with one another!

GROUP 2

bow, arrow, _____

lake, ocean, _____

shake, tremble, _____

GROUP 3

green, brown, _____

refrigerator, stove, _____

see, blink, _____

GROUP 4

sleet, hail, _____

hawk, pelican, _____

enemy, adversary, _____

GROUP 5

seven, twelve, _____

window, roof, _____

library, restaurant, _____

GROUP 6

grass, bush, _____

cricket, beetle, _____

shin, thigh, _____

FAST FINISHERS

Language Arts

Date _____

Name _____

A Question of Numbers

Maybe you've heard the expression "dressed to the nines." It means that a person is dressed up in fancy clothes to impress others. Many other common phrases have numbers in them. Each example below is missing a word. Only complete the expressions whose missing word is a number.

1. A cat has _____ lives.

2. Action speaks louder than _____.

3. _____ heads are better than one.

4. That's like the pot calling the kettle _____.

5. _____ wonders of the world.

6. The grass is always greener on the _____ side of the fence.

7. _____ corners of the Earth.

8. _____ 's company, _____ 's a crowd.

9. A stitch in time saves _____.

10. _____ is the best policy.

11. _____ days a week.

12. _____ is where the heart is.

YOUR TURN

Choose one phrase or quotation from the examples above that doesn't have a number in it. Complete the phrase with its missing word and write what you think the phrase means.

_____

_____

_____

FAST FINISHERS

Language Arts

Date _____

Name _____

Youth Sleuth

Surprise! It's your birthday and there's a batch of unsigned birthday cards on your desk at school. You know your classmates well enough to narrow the suspects down to six. Read their personality profiles in the box below. Then sign the name of the student on the card you think he or she sent.

> **Darren**—good at fixing things, likes music, rides a bicycle to school
> **Julia**—good at sports, likes history, has lived in several different cities
> **Mike**—good speller, plays piano, creates Web sites
> **Randi**—good artist, oldest girl in the class, collects seashells
> **Seth**—good at math, has a cat, eats lots of vegetables
> **Dara**—good photographer, always cheerful, likes science

Card 1.

Again I get to share your special day.
But for a change I will celebrate
Not with cookies and ice cream cake,
But peas and carrots on my plate
         Fondly,

_____

Card 2.

Happy birthday to my good friend!
I salute you with three cheers.
Did you know yours is the same
As a man named William Shakespeare's?
         Un abrazo,

_____

Card 3.

You may seem taller than Russell.
You may look more adult than Patty
You may be older than everyone else
But you'll never be older than me!
         A big fan,

_____

Card 4.

I thought about buying you a gift,
But I didn't know what you would like.
So instead I've decided to let you
Take a long ride on my new bike.
         Your friend,

_____

Card 5.

Finally your birthday has arrived!
Have you been thinking about it for a while?
I'm sure you'll spend the day as I do
Doing everything with a smile.
         Sincerely,

_____

Card 6.

Last year my birthday wishes were so big
They could've filled a whole CD-ROM.
This year they've gotten even bigger
So I'm posting them on
         www.haveahappy birthday.com!
         As always,

_____

FAST FINISHERS

Language Arts

The Million-Dollar Question

Imagine you're on a game show where the prize is a million dollars if you can get your partner to correctly guess a list of mystery items. You can use no more than five words in your description of each item. Below is the list of items you must get your partner to correctly identify. Circle the letter of the choice that you feel is the *most descriptive* of each word or phrase in bold face. We've done the first one for you.

1. **fork**

    a. has three prongs   b. kitchen item   c. usually with knife

2. **bicycle**

    a. method of transportation   b. has a place to sit   c. has two wheels

3. **grape**

    a. green or red   b. fruit on a vine   c. usually in a bunch

4. **paper clip**

    a. holds papers together   b. made of metal   c. office or school supply

5. **Web site**

    a. address on the Internet   b. seen on a computer   c. has many pages

6. **faucet**

    a. in every bathroom   b. water comes out of it   c. sometimes leaks

7. **thunder**

    a. weather occurrence   b. very loud   c. usually accompanies lightning

8. **fan**

    a. has blades   b. most run on electricity   c. circulates air to cool you

9. **polar bear**

    a. big and white   b. lives on land   c. large North Pole mammal

10. **parade**

    a. Fourth of July   b. marching band and floats   c. big crowds

FAST FINISHERS

Language Arts

Date _____

Name _____

Anagramania!

A word or phrase made by rearranging the letters in another word or phrase is called an anagram. For example, an anagram of *cars* is *scar*. If you rearrange the letters of *cartoon,* you get *no actor*. The letters in *United States* can become *a student site*.

Anagrams don't always make sense, but they always make real words. Look at the list of names below. Find each person's favorite by making an anagram using the letters in his or her name. Those with an asterisk (*) have two-word answers.

> **REMEMBER:** "A" and "an" are considered words!

PERSON	THEIR FAVORITE	ANAGRAM ANSWER
1. Debra	food	
2. Reed	animal	
3. Katie*	thing to use in a park	
4. Jonas	male name (besides his own)	
5. Gabriel*	pet	
6. Gary	color	
7. Curtis	type of fruit	
8. Lenny	female name	
9. Aaron*	part of a boat	
10. Miles	facial feature	

YOUR TURN

Choose a word (it doesn't have to be a name) and try to make an anagram out of it. See if your classmates can guess the word.

FAST FINISHERS

Language Arts

Date _____

Name _____

It's Raining Cats and Dogs

Each phrase below has a blank. Each blank can be filled in
with the name of an animal. Fill in the animal, then match
the phrase with its meaning in the center column and write
the correct letter in the right-hand column. For added fun,
look up the origin of each phrase in a book or online. We've done
the first one for you.

PHRASE	MEANING	CORRECT MATCH
1. ___*dog*___ days of summer	**a.** many choices	*i*
2. _____ got your tongue	**b.** hard-working person	
3. don't look a gift _____ in the mouth	**c.** vulnerable	
4. I'll be a _____'s uncle	**d.** unable to sit still	
5. sitting _____	**e.** can't speak	
6. eager _____	**f.** the first person always does well	
7. early bird catches the _____	**g.** a search for something difficult to find	
8. plenty of other _____ in the sea	**h.** don't complain about a present	
9. wild _____ chase	**i.** a hot period	
10. _____ in your pants	**j.** expression of surprise	

YOUR TURN

The title of this page is also a common expression. What do you think
it means?

FAST FINISHERS

Date _____

Name _____

Language Arts

Try This, Mate!

American and British people sometimes have different words or phrases for the same thing. For example, what Americans call a parking lot, the British call a car park. Below is a list of American and British terms. Draw a line to match each American term in the left column with its British counterpart in the right. Look up the words if you don't know.

AMERICAN	BRITISH
1. French fries	**a.** boot
2. mail	**b.** trainers
3. subway	**c.** dustbin
4. line	**d.** chips
5. apartment	**e.** bobby
6. sneakers	**f.** flat
7. friend	**g.** coach
8. diapers	**h.** bloke
9. trash can	**i.** crisps
10. elevator	**j.** nappies
11. guy	**k.** queue
12. police officer	**l.** mate
13. trunk (of car)	**m.** post
14. bus	**n.** tube
15. potato chips	**o.** lift

FAST FINISHERS

Language Arts

Word Twister

Each row of letters in column A is actually one of the phrases in column B all mixed up and smushed together. Draw a line from column A to column B and match the row with the phrase. There is only one correct match for each.

COLUMN A

1. vorscrgenefenearsaouaydos

2. hcosanrseteeretffrmtoheteest

3. kwatietitnllleintwesrtlk

4. yelytntoedadebaarlosirer

5. cnvperroeersiltivlkmy

6. tchebdasrrlthwiroacyeme

7. boaoworoyurwortwr

8. dileagelehgiaettenflglocap

9. bbacyiabtntheeeroptrkoey

10. bnhtmeidilreeoehwrhtenuys

COLUMN B

a. Row row row your boat

b. Rockabye baby, in the treetop

c. Early to bed and early to rise

d. Early bird catches the worm

e. Three blind mice, see how they run

f. I pledge allegiance to the flag

g. Never cry over spilt milk

h. Can't see the forest for the trees

i. Twinkle twinkle little star

j. Four score and seven years ago

YOUR TURN

Describe the strategy you used to figure out these word twisters.

_____

_____

_____

FAST FINISHERS

Language Arts

Date _____

Name _____

In Hiding

Amanda wrote ten silly sentences and hid one of her favorite things in each sentence. The favorites are hidden as the first letters of each word in the sentence, or the second letters, or the third, fourth, fifth or sixth letters—but they're always in the same position in each word. Find Amanda's favorites in each silly sentence below. The first one is done for you.

HINT: The favorites are not related to the silly sentences.

SILLY SENTENCE	FAVORITE	HIDDEN WORD	WHICH LETTER
1. Eggplants are easily upgraded vegetables.	fruit	*grape*	*2nd*
2. His allowance looks less overpaid when expense exceeds need.	holiday		
3. Short furry beasts can't argue there.	color		
4. Tired students treated their rational cousins politely.	city		
5. Can older users simply injure nature?	family member		
6. Each helicopter's person must throw fearless plays.	school subject		
7. Accept individuals having independent dinners.	animal		
8. Hiccups cause happy accidents that take precedence.	dessert		
9. Saturday every fun concept flings festively.	sport		
10. Cats run straight but smell uneven.	season		

YOUR TURN

Create your own silly sentence to hide one of your favorite things. See if your classmates can guess what it is.

FAST FINISHERS

Language Arts

Date _____

Name _____

Words in the Round

Each ring of letters below spells out a word. The letters are in order, either clockwise or counterclockwise—you just have to figure out where the word starts! Write your answers in the blanks.

1.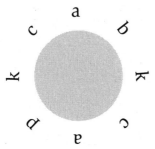

_____

2.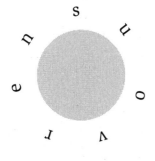

_____

3.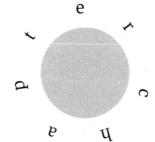

_____

4.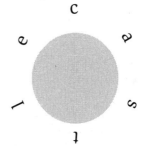

_____

5.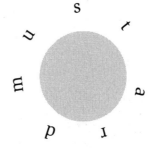

_____

6.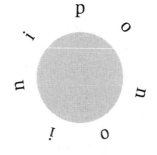

_____

YOUR TURN

Create your own "word in the round" and ask a friend or family member to determine what the word is.

FAST FINISHERS

Language Arts

Date _____

Name _____

Crabby Abby

Each sentence below is hiding the speaker's name. The letters of the name are in a row. When you figure out which words and letters reveal the name, underline them. Then write the name on the line. We've done the first one for you.

1. I saw a big cr<u>ab by</u> the lifeguard stand. ____*Abby*____

2. It looks like it will be another gray Monday. _____

3. How can new students adjust to a school and its

    routines quickly? _____

4. At dinner, we all want to tell entertaining stories. _____

5. After a hard day, the mules lie down to rest. _____

6. Please be kind and rewind all videotapes before

    returning them. _____

7. Tell Simon I care about helping the whales. _____

8. The wolves around here howl in darkness. _____

9. The TV show was comical and sad at the same time. _____

10. The fox den is entirely hidden beneath a pile of leaves. _____

YOUR TURN

Try to create a sentence in which your name is hidden. Warning: It is hard to do this with MOST names!

50

FAST FINISHERS

Language Arts

Date _____

Name _____

Are Fries French?

The names of many common items include a country. Sometimes the item is from that country, but many times it's not. Match each country with the word in the item column that goes with it by writing its letter on the blank line. There is one correct country for each.

COUNTRY	ITEM
1. French _____	**a.** taffy
2. India _____	**b.** channel
3. Canadian _____	**c.** measles
4. German _____	**d.** terrier
5. Chinese _____	**e.** beetle
6. American _____	**f.** checkers
7. Scottish _____	**g.** toast
8. English _____	**h.** goose
9. Turkish _____	**i.** pie
10. Japanese _____	**j.** ink

YOUR TURN

Think of other phrases or items that begin with a country. You may repeat a country.

FAST FINISHERS

Language Arts

Date _____

Name _____

The Inside Story

Each word on the list below is either hiding another word from the list within it or is hidden within another word from the list. For example, the word *maple* is hidden inside the word *example*, once you rearrange and discard certain letters. As a result, *maple* is written in the first column next to *example*. When you get to the word *maple* further down the list, you'll find no words from the list hiding within it. But *maple* was hidden inside the word *example*, so *example* is written in the second column. Look at the other words in the list. Decide whether they belong in the first or the second column. Good luck!

HINT: In most cases, hidden words are not related to the words in which they are hidden.

WORD LIST	WHAT WORD IS HIDDEN INSIDE?	WHAT WORD IS IT HIDDEN INSIDE?
1. example	*maple*	
2. broom		
3. slippery		
4. scarecrow		
5. stole		
6. bookmark		
7. voter		
8. piles		
9. races		
10. lighthouse		
11. goal		
12. maple		*example*
13. logical		
14. government		

Activities for Fast Finishers: Language Arts Scholastic Professional Books

Date _____

Name _____

Three's Company . . .

You know the old saying: Two's company, three's a crowd. For the words on this page, though, we might say three's company, four's a crowd. Each word in bold is followed by four more words. Three of them can be formed using letters from the boldface word. But one of them is an impostor and doesn't belong to the group. Circle the one word that *can't* be formed from the letters in the bold-face word.

TIP: The three words that belong to the group don't need to use all the letters from the bold-face word, but they can't repeat or add any letters either.

1. **glacier**	real	crier	glare	clear
2. **umbrella**	mule	lumber	label	alarm
3. **sideways**	shady	weds	daisy	sways
4. **abbreviation**	orbit	invite	never	native
5. **lifeguard**	figure	fudge	finger	fluid
6. **opportunity**	potion	turnip	unity	prior
7. **spaghetti**	pasty	eight	pigs	gates
8. **reflection**	recent	renter	force	client

YOUR TURN

Pick a word and form three smaller words from it. Throw in a fourth word that can't be made from its letters and ask a friend or family member to spot the impostor!

_____

_____   _____   _____   _____

FAST FINISHERS

Language Arts

Date _____

Name _____

Animal Scramble

Each animal name below has been cleverly disguised.
It's either a *jumbled* word (owc = cow), a word in
which each letter is one *behind* in the alphabet
(cow = dpx), or a word in which each letter is one
ahead in the alphabet (cow = bnv). Tell which method
was used to disguise the word, then write each
unscrambled word in the chart below.

DISGUISED ANIMAL	UNSCRAMBLED	WHICH METHOD?
1. cbu		
2. grof		
3. rgddo		
4. tlvol		
5. wheal		
6. dspdpejmf		
7. lnmjdx		
8. frigaef		
9. cfbwfs		
10. noonrtl		

YOUR TURN

Pick two other animals and disguise their names in each of these
three ways.

_____ _____ _____

_____ _____ _____

FAST FINISHERS

Language Arts

Date _____

Name _____

On the Double!

Each word in column 1 has a match with a word in column 2 based on two criteria. One is categorical (having to do with groups) and the other is linguistic (having to do with language). On the lines, write the letter of the word in column 2 that has a "double" match with the word in column 1 and give two reasons for choosing it. We've done the first one for you.

TIP: Not every word in column 2 has a match.

COLUMN 1	COLUMN 2	CATEGORICAL REASON	LINGUISTIC REASON
1. pear _M_	A. iron	*both are fruits*	*both begin with "p"*
	B. red		
2. road ____	C. gold		
	D. blue		
3. eagle ____	E. lane	_____	_____
	F. owl		
4. talk ____	G. street	_____	_____
	H. plane		
5. copper ____	I. read	_____	_____
	J. car		
6. train ____	K. sip		
	L. parrot		
	M. pineapple		
7. black ____	N. bread	_____	_____
	O. yellow		
8. cheese ____	P. stale	_____	_____

YOUR TURN

Write your own double match list and try it out on a friend or family member!

FAST FINISHERS

Language Arts

Call the Dog

Marvin wants to name his new puppy with a word that doesn't contain any letters found in the names of his other pets. He knows this means he may end up with a strangely named dog. Write the letters Marvin can and can't use. Then, circle any name on Marvin's list that would work.

Marvin's other pet names:

goldfish – Twitch   cat – Bobo   bird – Loonin   snake – Whip

MARVIN'S LIST OF POSSIBLE DOG NAMES	LETTERS MARVIN CAN'T USE	LETTERS MARVIN CAN USE
Sammy		
King		
Sara		
Joker		
Frazz		
Rex		
Waffle		
Sarah		
Eek		
Murky		
Queen		
Rave		

YOUR TURN

Find or create two more names that Marvin could use for his dog.

FAST FINISHERS

Language Arts

Date _____

Name _____

Top of the Morning!

Circle all of the following words that form a common word or phrase with the word "top." Write the words or phrases on the lines provided.

TIP: "Top" can come either before or after the word or phrase.

1. hat _____

2. banana _____

3. tap _____

4. big _____

5. speed _____

6. stop _____

7. story _____

8. ten _____

9. end _____

10. floor _____

11. dog _____

12. drawer _____

YOUR TURN

Create a similar list for the word "big" and try it with classmates.

FAST FINISHERS

Language Arts

Date _____

Name _____

Word Train

Below are ten sets of random words. Arrange each set of words so that the last letter of the word is the same as the first letter of the next word. We've done the first one for you.

1. drama, apple, ripcord, enter, artery ➡ *apple, enter, ripcord, drama, artery*

2. especially, lozenge, seesaw, tinsel, worrywart ➡ _____

3. everywhere, disco, licorice, grateful, oblong ➡ _____

4. elf, spinning, nightingale, frozen, gentle ➡ _____

5. kennel, exact, loan, dusk, nimble ➡ _____

6. dodo, outrageous, princess, pulp, slip ➡ _____

7. turnstile, elegant, sandbar, tease, racquet ➡ _____

8. mammal, dentist, loose, emblem, tricycle ➡ _____

9. manipulate, react, estimate, turtle, eardrum, writer ➡ _____

10. yellow, difficulty, donor, wandered, rewind ➡ _____

YOUR TURN

Write a six-word chain in which the last letter of each word is the same as the beginning letter of the next word.

_____ _____ _____ _____ _____ _____

Activities for Fast Finishers: Language Arts   Scholastic Professional Books

FAST FINISHERS

Language Arts

Date _____

Name _____

All Locked In

Some countries or bodies of water, such as lakes, are often described as landlocked. That means they are completely surrounded by land and do not touch oceans or seas. What if a vowel were completely surrounded by consonants? Although it is not a real term, that condition might be described as "consonant locked." Look at the list below. Put an X in the box next to any word in which *all* of the vowels are locked in by consonants.

HINT: Do not count "y" as a vowel. If two vowels are next to each other, they are considered consonant locked.

1. marry	❑	9. oblong	❑
2. eel	❑	10. rewind	❑
3. psychic	❑	11. switcheroo	❑
4. spoon	❑	12. highlight	❑
5. empire	❑	13. barricade	❑
6. lasso	❑	14. speedometer	❑
7. grain	❑	15. postpone	❑
8. blackboard	❑	16. literally	❑

YOUR TURN

Is your first or last name consonant locked? How about the name of your school? Think of three more words that are consonant locked.

_____

_____

_____

_____

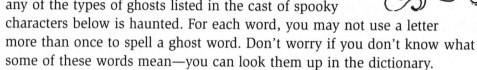

Date _____

Name _____

Language Arts

FAST FINISHERS

Haunted Words

Which of the words on the list below are haunted?
Only the ones that have a ghost of some kind hiding
within them! Any word that contains all the letters of
any of the types of ghosts listed in the cast of spooky
characters below is haunted. For each word, you may not use a letter
more than once to spell a ghost word. Don't worry if you don't know what
some of these words mean—you can look them up in the dictionary.

THE CAST OF SPOOKY CHARACTERS
ghost   phantom   spook   spirit   specter

WORD LIST	SPOOKY CHARACTER FOUND INSIDE
1. Goths	_____
2. photojournalism	_____
3. triskaidekaphobia	_____
4. interdisciplinary	_____
5. sarcophagus	_____
6. respiration	_____
7. metamorphosis	_____
8. striping	_____
9. respectful	_____
10. photodisintegration	_____
11. goulash	_____
12. spectator	_____
13. thoroughness	_____
14. spokeswoman	_____

Activities for Fast Finishers: Language Arts   Scholastic Professional Books

ANSWERS

Page 6: Read, Write and Solve!
tool/chisel; **water**/geyser;
clothing/leotard; **star**/nova;
house/bungalow; **color**/ivory;
sound/thud; **bird**/ostrich
1. b u n g a l o w 2. i v o r y
3. l e o t a r d 4. g **e** y s e r
5. o s t r **i** c h 6. n o v **a**
7. t h u d 8. c h i s e **l**
Puzzle Answer: *literate*

Page 7: Which Is Which?
The following words should be
circled: 1. draw 2. show 3. exit
4. plot 5. park 6. loan 7. hide 8. find
9. sail 10. take 11. record

Page 8: Get in on the Action
The following words should be circled:
2. sat, chirp, fly 3. stop, move
4. name, named, will buy 5. close,
shut 6. enjoy 7. hear, feel 8. start,
extinguish, prevent 9. believe 10.
played, cavorted

Page 9: Whisper or YELL?
Quiet words: whisper, mumble,
mutter, murmur **Loud words:** yell,
scream, shout, demand

QUIET WORD FIND

```
W H I S P E D m o
w a h r D e a e M
h m u r m u r m C
i u e m u t t m U
s t M U T T E b R
p t m u r m r l M
e e m u m b l e U
r r Y u e s M u R
```

LOUD WORD FIND

```
T Y E s c r e a r
S H C O U T S C e
S a Y E L L T o S
H s S l l e s e C
O P S H O U T a R
U S R E y e m l E
R D E M A N D s A
Y E u y I o o u M
```

Page 10: What the Action Is
2. B (window can't see) 3. D (tree
can't chop) 4. A (hand can't stand)
5. D (star can't visit) 6. C (dog can't
throw) 7. C (horse can't trade) 8. C
(athlete can't foot) 9. A (driver can't
sputter) 10. D (asphalt can't pave)

Page 11: Can the Cat Act?
Missing nouns and verbs are as follows:
1. pets 2. flow 3. hops 4. team
5. react 6. singer 7. sobs 8. resist
9. painter 10. pots

Page 12: Where's the Me?
1. Evelyn jumped after (he, she, **I**)
accidentally slammed the door. 2.
Jackson couldn't predict how much
snow (he, she, **I**) would have to shovel after the storm. 3. Please help (her,
him, **me**) clean the house. 4. Molly's
favorite color is blue, but most of
(**her**) clothes are red. 5. (**I**) don't
know any secrets, but I wish I did.
6. Twenty students appeared in the
school play and performed (**their**)
roles perfectly. 7. The teacher saw
you do (**it**). 8. Her sandwich is much
thicker than (**theirs**) because of the
homemade bread. 9. If these instruments aren't hers, then they must be
(**theirs**). 10. You knitted (me, him,
her) a cashmere sweater?

Page 13: Inspecting Adjectives
The following words should be
eliminated:
2. speak 3. shine 4. direction
5. trip 6. paragraph 7. building
8. space 9. when 10. crease

Page 14: X Marks the Adjective
The following nouns in parentheses
should be marked with an "x" on the
chart for each adjective:
inexpensive (book, dinner); **green**
(vine); **long** (street, book, dinner,
vine); **frightened** (skunk, friend);
hungry (skunk, friend); **ancient**
(street, book, castle, vine); **confusing**
(book); **clever** (book, friend); **private**
(street, dinner, castle); **mysterious**
(street, book, friend, castle) (If students have other answers not shown,
ask them to explain them.)

Page 15: The Difficul-test Activity
2. more sunny, alternative: sunnier
3. importantest, correction: most
important 4. playfulest, correction:
most playful 5. more green, alternative: greener 6. more colorful, correction: most colorful 7. most deep,
alternative: deepest 8. fastest, correction: faster 9. preparedest, correction:
most prepared 10. more close, alternative: closer 11. farther, correction: far-
thest 12. more smarter, correction:
smarter

Page 16: An Adverbially Tricky Code
2. fully 3. playfully 4. brilliantly
5. hysterically 6. finally 7. loyally
8. skillfully 9. practically
10. hypnotically

Page 17: Punctuation Situation
A comma, colon, or quotation marks
should be inserted where shaded in
these sentences:
1. Jack needed help building a bookcase, so I said, "I'll be right over!" He
asked me to bring the following: a
screwdriver, a hammer, and a box of
nails. 2. On hot days, only one thing
would stop us from going to the
beach: crowds. Of course, rain might
also keep us away. 3. The letter
began, "Dear Mr. President: Thank
you for your support." 4. "I heard a
strange, scary howl last night," I told
my friend Jack over the telephone. "I
know it sounds crazy, but I swear it
sounded just like a werewolf!"
5. "The line-up for tonight's show will
be as follows: Brenda the wonder
frog, Tulip the talking toucan, and
Henrietta the hip hippo," the talk-
show host said while looking into the
television camera. 6. It's 3:00 P.M.
This is when I usually like to snack
on a piece of pecan pie and have a
cup of tea. However, today I don't
want any. 7. At the rehearsal, the conductor gave us this schedule: chorus
meets every Tuesday, band rehearsal
is on Wednesday, and individual practice sessions meet on Thursday.
8. "Remember this old saying: An
apple a day keeps the doctor away,"
the doctor told the little girl after the
check-up. 9. Houston, Dallas, and San
Antonio are all major cities. However,
much of Texas is still made up of
wide-open spaces. 10. The day of the
race felt like this: sunny and spectacular. Even so, few people turned out
to run.

Page 18: A Highly Irregular Rhyme
Irregular verbs should be crossed out
and corrected as follows:
Stanza one: *flied* becomes *flew*,
knowed becomes *knew* **Stanza two:**
slided becomes *slid*, *hided* becomes
hid **Stanza three:** *creeped* becomes
crept, *keeped* becomes *kept* **Stanza
four:** *shaked* becomes *shook*, *taked*
becomes *took* **Stanza five:** *bended*
becomes *bent*, *goed* becomes *went*
Stanza six: *awaked* becomes *awoke*,
speaked becomes *spoke* **Stanza seven:**
catched becomes *caught*, *teached*
becomes *taught*

Page 19: Sentence the Make
The correct order is as follows:
1. My dog barks at passing cars.
2. You have a nice family. 3. The penguins are the newest animals at the zoo. ALSO ACCEPTABLE: At the zoo, the penguins are the newest animals.
4. Speak louder so everyone can hear you. 5. My grandfather was a boy when he got this clock. ALSO ACCEPTABLE: When he got this clock, my grandfather was a boy.
6. I'm better at math than I was last year. 7. Thank you for being a good friend. 8. The pitcher gave us free tickets to the next game. 9. My father's dream for me is to be an air force pilot. 10. Frank's shirt was as wrinkled as a raisin.

Page 20: Places Trading
1. splattered 2. milk 3. magazines
4. caught 5. umbrellas 6. show
7. urge 8. telescope 9. book
10. pizza

Page 21: Three Likes and You're Out
Adele didn't strike out. She used "like" incorrectly exactly three times, so she just made the grade. Correct uses are in boldface and incorrect uses are circled.

Unlike the rest of my family, I never **liked** camping much—until this summer. I was forced to go on a three-day hiking and camping trip. Of course I expected it to be, (like,) the worst weekend of my life. I tried to get out of it but my mom didn't **like** that very much. "**Like** it or not, you are coming on this trip!" she said, smiling.

Once there, I started to feel differently. The forest had such a fresh scent, **like** nothing else I've ever smelled. I **liked** the sound of the babbling brooks. Every so often we sat on rocks to rest. Once, one of the rocks was, (like,) hot as if it had been in a fire—my dad jumped up as soon as he sat down!

At night, everything was so tranquil. When I heard a strange rustling noise in nearby bushes, I was, (like,) a little afraid, but it soon went away. We all slept very peacefully. A year ago I **disliked** camping, but now I say there is nothing **like** spending a warm night under the stars.

Page 22: Turn! Run! Break! Fly!
The best pair of matches are as follows:

1. **turn** on shower; turn into driveway, turn up volume, turn over blanket 2. **run** through choices; run over nails; run up stairs; run across mistakes 3. **break** into laughter; break down wall; break up mob; break through ice 4. **fly** off handle; fly in style; fly into sunset; fly by night

Page 23: Language Arts Smarts
The following should be crossed out:
1. cower (Cower is a verb.) 2. goose (should be lower case since the portion following the colon isn't a complete sentence.) 3. correct
4. comma (The comma is a punctuation mark.) 5. Viking (Viking should be capitalized because it is a proper name.) 6. except for the letter Y (Y can serve as both a vowel and a consonant.) 7. correct 8. serialized, anesthetized (Serialized and anesthetized don't refer to milk.)
9. I (I isn't a consonant) 10. correct

Page 24: One Letter Short
The following underlined letters in boldface are missing from these words and should appear in the right-hand column of the chart:
1. ja**c**kals 2. r**o**ute 3. Jura**ss**ic
4. citizen**s** 5. ex**c**ept 6. Ji**tt**ery
7. baz**a**ar 8. book**k**eeper

Page 25: A Misspell Spell
2. Open 24 Hours (e became a, o became i, u became e) 3. One size fits all (a became u, e became o, i became a, o became e) 4. Please drive carefully (a became e, e became i, i became o, u became a) 5. Anniversary sale (a became o, e became a, i became u) 6. Ticket window (e became o, i became a, o became u) 7. Welcome to our school (e became u, o became i, u became o) 8. Keep your town clean (a became o, e became u, o became e, u became i) 9. Fixed while you wait (a became o, e became u, i became a, o became e, u became i) 10. Work zone (o became a, e became i)

Page 26: Letter Twins Go Missing
The following letters are missing and, when added, spell the following words:
D–disappeared 2. T–trait 3. N–nation
4. E–escape 5. W–willow
6. M–mainstream 7. R–reviver
8. C–cinematic 9. C–civic
10. D & T–dread, treat 11. K–kayak
12. M– madam
Your Turn: The palindromes are reviver, civic, kayak, and madam

Page 27: Strange Spelling Bee
Correctly spelled words and ranks are as follows:
dunjeon: dungeon, 4th letter
absense: absence, 6th letter
associatian: association, 10th letter
governer, governor, 7th letter
correspondance, correspondence; 11th letter
emphibian, amphibian, 1st letter
environmentul, environmental, 12th letter
thesauris, thesaurus, 8th letter
boomarang, boomerang, 5th letter
chlorophill, chlorophyll, 9th letter
nesessary, necessary, 3rd letter

Page 28: Between the Lines
The following words are spelled correctly: *heyday, yearn, dumbfounded, rancid, naïve, drivel, plunder, nymph, lexicon.* They should be inserted into the rows in this order:
P L U N D E R A N C
I D U M B F O U N D
E D R I V E L E X I
C O N Y M P H E Y D
A Y E A R N A I V E

Page 29: No Nonsense!
When you replace the vowels with "o," the following words would be in the blanks:
1. rose (*Floor, word, moon* are words. *Roso* is not.) 2. oboe (*Born, crook, flop* are words. *Oboo* is not.) 3. open (*Most, polo, toll* are words. *Opon* is not.) 4. plant (*Gross, wood, form* are words. *Plont* is not.) 5. snap (*Clock, knock, blob* are words. *Snop* is not.)
6. sent (*Lost, song, pots* are words. *Sont* is not.) 7. trail (*Loop, soy, poor* are words. *Trool* is not.) 8. button (*Roof, most, root* are words. *Botton* is not.) 9. finale (*Noon, rode, stool* are words. *Fonolo* is not.) 10. ugly (*Too, typo, shop* are words. *Ogly* is not.)

Page 30: Like Two Peas in a Pod
2. riot, root 3. seat, soot 4. lair, leer, liar 5. moot, meat 6. duel, deal, dual, dial 7. seep, soup, soap 8. tied, toad, 9. pool, peel, pail 10. deed, died, dead 11. toil, tail 12. mean, moon, main 13. seam 14. pear, poor, peer 15. rear

Page 31: Animal Spies
The following animals are hidden if you remove these words in parentheses:
2. weasel (narwhal, grasshopper)
3. pelican (lion or louse, giraffe)
4. gazelle (ibis, armadillo)
5. porcupine (moth, anteater)
6. cricket (snake, coyote)
7. ostrich (toucan, sheep)
8. salamander (spider, muskrat or manatee)
9. lobster (python, wombat)
10. mole (aardvark, fox)

Page 32: E-I-E-I-O
These words are formed when you unscramble and add double vowels:
2. moon 3. seem 4. eerie 5. igloo 6. school 7. spooky 8. kneeling; 9. oodles 10. skiing 11. queen 12. hawaii

Page 33: A Classics Problem
The following are the original book titles; corrected misspellings in new titles are in parentheses:
2. *The Cricket in Times Square* (Site)
3. *Little House on the Prairie* (Residence) 4. *Where the Wild Things Are* (Well-behaved) 5. *The Lion, the Witch, and the Wardrobe* (Supernatural) 6. *Goodnight Moon* (Satellite) 7. *The Very Hungry Caterpillar* (Appetite) 8. *The Little Engine That Could* (Locomotive) 9. *The Snowy Day* (Precipitation) 10. *The Giving Tree* (Generous) 11. *Guess How Much I Love You* (Affection) 12. *The Polar Express* (Arctic)

Page 34: Double Take
1. bb: bubble 2. cc: account 3. dd, zz: puddle, puzzle 4. ee: jeer 5. bb, ff, tt: babble, baffle, battle 6. dd, ff: odd, off 7. pp, tt, nn: sipping, sitting, sinning 8. ll, nn, rr, ss, zz: fully, funny, furry, fussy, fuzzy 9. ee, oo: peel, pool 10. bb, gg, rr: ebb, egg, err

Page 35: Letter Lottery
The following correct letters form these words:
2. K, speak or peaks 3. R, chore 4. E, maple or ample 5. N, wrong or grown 6. S, flash 7. L, spill or pills 8. R, color 9. V, drive 10. G, gargle

Page 36: Pieces of Pie
2. k/ey li/me or pu/m/pk/in
3. bl/ue/be/rr/y or st/ra/wb/er/ry
4. Bo/st/on cr/e/am
5. k/ey li/me or pu/m/pk/in
6. bl/ue/be/rr/y or st/ra/wb/er/ry

Page 37: Double Check
Misspelled words the computer missed are as follows:
1. mussel/muscle; pride/pried
2. lesson/lesson
3. rein/reign 4. yolks/yokes
5. stationery/stationary; knead/need
6. turns/terns 7. fined/find; peace/piece; medal/metal 8. complement/compliment 9. currents/currants; sent/scent
10. core/corps; moor/more

Page 38: Word Magic
2. garden, danger 3. deer, reed
4. ocean, canoe 5. keep, peek 6. react, crate 7. stone, notes 8. net, ten
9. ignore, region 10. rats, star

p	v	b	o	l	e	g	e	n	d	a		
h	f	a	f	o	o	t	p	x	t			
a		s	f	o	t	p	r	w	c			
n	s	z	f	s	l	e	u	t	h	i	o	
t	o	o	e	m	a	g	l	p	s			
o	t	o	n	t	i	h	t	w				
m	a	s	t	r	a	n	g	e	o	n	a	
n	d	p	a	t	w	m	s	d	a			
s	r	p	p	e	y	t						
g	m	b	i	t	i	n	p	e	t			
h	a	o	n	j	u	c	o	s	l			
g	k	t	v	r	o	t	m					
i	t	w	t	t	c							
c	o	b	w	e	b	s	t	e	r	o		
l	e	d	n	s	p	o	o	k	y			

Page 39: Word Hide
Page 40: Rhyme is Reason
Group 2: quiver, river, shiver **Group 3:** pink, sink, wink **Group 4:** snow, crow, foe **Group 5:** four, door or floor, store **Group 6:** tree or pea, bee or flea, knee

Page 41: A Question of Numbers
The following phrases contain numbers: 1. cat has **nine** lives 3. **Two** heads are better than one 5. **seven** wonders of the world 7. **four** corners of the Earth 8. **Two's** company, **three's** a crowd 9. A stitch in time saves **nine** 11. **Seven** days a week

Page 42: Youth Sleuth
Card 1: Seth **Card 2:** Julia **Card 3:** Randi **Card 4:** Darren **Card 5:** Dara **Card 6:** Mike

Page 43: The Million-Dollar Question
2. a. 2 points, b. 1 point, c. 3 points
3. a. 1 point, b. 2 points, c. 3 points
4. a. 3 points, b. 1 point, c. 2 points
5. a. 3 points, b. 2 points, c. 1 point
6. a. 2 points, b. 3 points, c. 1 point
7. a. 2 points, b. 1 point, c. 3 points
8. a. 2 points, b. 1 point, c. 3 points
9. a. 2 points, b. 1 point, c. 3 points
10. a. 2 points, b. 3 points, c. 1 point

Page 44: Anagramania!
1. bread 2. deer 3. a kite 4. Jason
5. a gerbil 6. gray 7. citrus 8. Lynne
9. an oar 10. smile

Page 45: It's Raining Cats and Dogs
1. dog; i 2. cat; e 3. horse; h
4. monkey; j 5. duck; c 6. beaver; b
7. worm; f 8. fish; a 9. goose; g
10. ant; d
Your Turn: "It's raining cats and dogs," means it's raining very hard.

Page 46: Try This, Mate!
1. d 2. m 3. n 4. k 5. f 6. b 7. l 8. j
9. c 10. o 11. h 12. e 13. a 14. g 15. i

Page 47: Word Twister
1. j 2. h 3. i 4. c 5. g 6. d 7. a 8. f 9. b
10. e

Page 48: In Hiding
1. 2nd letter: grape 2. 1st letter: Halloween 3. 3rd letter: orange
4. 5th letter: Detroit 5. 1st letter: cousin
6. 4th letter: history
7. 6th letter: tiger 8. 3rd letter: cupcake
9. 3rd letter: tennis
10. 2nd letter: autumn

Page 49: Words in the Round
1. backpack 2. nervous 3. chapter
4. mustard 5. castle 6. opinion

Page 50: Crabby Abby
2. **gray Mond**ay—Raymond
3. **can ne**w—Anne
4. **tell en**tertaining—Ellen
5. **mu**le**s lie**—Leslie
6. **and rew**ind—Andrew
7. Si**mon I car**e—Monica
8. howl **in da**rkness—Linda
9. comic**al and**—Alan
10. **den is e**ntirely—Denise

Page 51: **Are Fries French?**
1. g 2. j 3. h 4. c 5. f 6. i 7. d 8. b
9. a 10. e
Your Turn: Answers may vary.

Page 52: **The Inside Story**
The following words should appear
in the first column 1. *maple* 3. *piles*
4. *races* 6. *broom* 10. *stole* 13. *goal*
14. *voter*
The following words should appear in
the second column 2. *bookmark*
(because *broom* is hidden inside it);
5. *lighthouse* 7. *government*
8. *slippery* 9. *scarecrow* 11. *logical*
12. *example*

Page 53: **Three's Company...**
1. crier 2. alarm 3. shady 4. never
5. finger 6. prior 7. pasty 8. renter

Page 54: **Animal Scramble**
1. bat (behind) 2. frog (jumbled)
3. sheep (ahead) 4. skunk (behind)
5. whale (jumbled) 6. crocodile
(behind) 7. monkey (ahead) 8. giraffe
(jumbled) 9. beaver (behind)
10. opossum (ahead)

Page 55: **On the Double!**
Accept all reasonable answers.
Possible answers are:
2. E (places to drive on/both have
four letters) 3. F (both are birds/both
begin with vowels) 4. K (actions
mouths do/both are verbs) 5. A (both
are metals/both are two-syllable
words) 6. H (both are ways to trav-
el/both rhyme) 7. D (both are col-
ors/both begin with "b") 8. N (both
are edible/ both are one-syllable
words)

Page 56: **Call the Dog**
Names That Would Work: Sammy,
Sara, Frazz, Rex, Eek, Murky, Rave

Page 57: **Top of the Morning!**
The following words and phrases can
be made with top: top *hat*, top
banana, big *top*, top *speed*, top *story*,
top *ten*, top *floor*, top *dog*, top
drawer. The words *tap, stop,* and *end*
should not be circled.

Page 58: **Word Train**
2. seesaw, worrywart, tinsel, lozenge,
especially 3. disco, oblong, grateful,
licorice, everywhere 4. spinning,
gentle, elf, frozen, nightingale
5. dusk, kennel, loan, nimble, exact
6. dodo, outrageous, slip, pulp,
princess 7. sandbar, racquet, tease,
elegant, turnstile 8. dentist, tricycle,
emblem, mammal, loose 9. writer,
react, turtle, eardrum, manipulate,
estimate 10. rewind, difficulty,
yellow, wandered, donor *or* donor,
rewind, difficulty, yellow, wandered
or difficulty, yellow, wandered, donor,
rewind *or* wandered, donor, rewind,
difficulty, yellow *or* yellow, wandered,
donor, rewind, difficulty

Page 59: **All Locked In**
The following words should be
marked: 1. marry 3. psychic 4. spoon
7. grain 8. blackboard 10. rewind 12.
highlight 14. speedometer 16. literally

Page 60: **Haunted Words**
1. Goths—ghost 2. photojournalism—
phantom 3. triskaidekaphobia—spirit
4. interdisciplinary—spirit 6. respira-
tion—spirit 8. striping—spirit
9. respectful—specter 10. photodisin-
tegration—spirit ghost 13. thorough-
ness—ghost 14. spokeswoman—
spook